A Quick Guide to…

Gender Mainstreaming in Finance

Gita Sen

Commonwealth Secretariat

Gender Management System Series

Gender Management System Handbook

Using Gender-Sensitive Indicators: A Reference Manual for Governments and Other Stakeholders

Gender Mainstreaming in Development Planning: A Reference Manual for Governments and Other Stakeholders

Gender Mainstreaming in Finance: A Reference Manual for Governments and Other Stakeholders

Gender Mainstreaming in the Public Service: A Reference Manual for Governments and Other Stakeholders

Gender Mainstreaming in Education: A Reference Manual for Governments and Other Stakeholders

Gender Mainstreaming in Trade and Industry: A Reference Manual for Governments and Other Stakeholders

Gender Mainstreaming in Agriculture and Rural Development: A Reference Manual for Governments and Other Stakeholders

Gender Mainstreaming in Information and Communications: A Reference Manual for Governments and Other Stakeholders

Gender and Equal Employment Opportunities: A Reference Manual for Governments and Other Stakeholders

A Quick Guide to the Gender Management System

A Quick Guide to Using Gender-Sensitive Indicators

A Quick Guide to Gender Mainstreaming in Development Planning

A Quick Guide to Gender Mainstreaming in Finance

A Quick Guide to Gender Mainstreaming in the Public Service

A Quick Guide to Gender Mainstreaming in Education

A Quick Guide to Gender Mainstreaming in Trade and Industry

A Quick Guide to Gender Mainstreaming in Agriculture and Rural Development

A Quick Guide to Gender Mainstreaming in Information and Communications

A Quick Guide to Gender and Equal Employment Opportunities

Commonwealth Secretariat
Marlborough House
Pall Mall, London SW1Y 5HX,
United Kingdom

© Commonwealth Secretariat,
June 1999

Designed and published by the Commonwealth Secretariat.
Printed in the United Kingdom by Abacus Direct.
Wherever possible, the Commonwealth Secretariat uses paper sourced from sustainable forests or from sources that minimise a destructive impact on the environment.

Copies of this publication can be ordered direct from:

Vale Packaging Ltd,
420 Vale Road, Tonbridge, Kent
TN9 1TD, United Kingdom

Tel: + 44 (0)1732 359387
Fax: +44 (0) 1732 770620
e-mail: vale@vale-ltd.co.uk

Price: £5.99
0-85092-601-7

Web sites:
http://www.thecommonwealth.org/gender
http://www.thecommonwealth.org
http://www.youngcommonwealth.org

Contents

Preface

In 1996, Commonwealth Ministers Responsible for Women's Affairs mandated the Commonwealth Secretariat to develop the concept of the Gender Management System (GMS), a comprehensive network of structures, mechanisms and processes for bringing a gender perspective to bear in the mainstream of all government policies, programmes and projects. The success of the GMS depends upon a broad-based partnership in society in which government consults and acts co-operatively with the other key stakeholders, who include civil society and the private sector. The establishment and strengthening of gender management systems and of national women's machineries was the first of 15 government action points identified in the 1995 Commonwealth Plan of Action on Gender and Development.

This guide is intended to assist readers in using a GMS to mainstream gender in the finance ministry of national governments. It is an abridged version of the GMS publication *Gender Mainstreaming in Finance: A Reference Manual for Governments and Other Stakeholders* presenting the main points of that document in an accessible way. It is hoped that both documents will be used by policy-makers, personnel managers, planners and others.

These publications are part of the Gender Management System Series, which provides tools and sector-specific guidelines for gender mainstreaming. This guide is intended to be used in combination with the other documents in the Gender Management System Series, particularly the *Gender Management System Handbook* which presents the conceptual and methodological framework of the GMS.

The development of the Gender Management System Reference Manuals and Quick Guides has been a collaborative effort between the Commonwealth Secretariat's Gender and Youth Affairs Division and many individuals and groups. Their contributions to the thinking behind the GMS are gratefully acknowledged. In particular, I would like to mention the following: all those member governments who supported the development of the GMS and encouraged us to move the project forward; participants at the first GMS meeting in Britain in February 1997 and at the GMS Workshop in Malta in April 1998, who provided invaluable conceptual input and feedback; the Steering Committee on the Plan of Action (SCOPA). I am also most grateful to: Gita Sen of the Indian Institute of Management, who wrote the text of this guide, and Daniel Woolford, Consultant Editor of the GMS Series, who edited it, and the staff of the Gender Affairs Department, Gender and Youth Affairs Division, Commonwealth Secretariat, particularly Ms Eleni Stamiris, former Director of the Division, who took the lead in formulating the GMS concept and mobilising the various stakeholders in its development, Dr Judith May-Parker who provided substantive editorial input, and Dr Rawwida Baksh-Soodeen, Project Co-ordinator of the Gender Management System Series, who guided the project through to publication.

We hope that this resource series will be of genuine use to you in your efforts to mainstream gender.

Nancy Spence
Director
Gender and Youth Affairs Division
Commonwealth Secretariat

1 Introduction

Although the historical antecedents of modern-day women's movements go back at least to the previous century, particular attention has been paid during the last three decades to the concerns of women in the development process. Starting with the pioneering effort of Ester Boserup (1970), considerable effort has been expended by researchers, activists and policy-makers in analysing gender relations in the context of development, in understanding their practical consequences for women and men, and drawing out the policy implications thereof.

Defining Gender

Gender can be defined as the set of characteristics, roles and behaviour patterns that distinguish women from men which are constructed not biologically but socially and culturally. The sex of an individual is biologically determined, whereas gender characteristics are socially constructed, a product of nurturing, conditioning, and socio-cultural norms and expectations. These characteristics change over time and from one culture to another. The concept of gender refers not only to women and men but, importantly to the relations of power between them. Gender relations are constantly being renegotiated in the context of changing political, economic, social, and cultural environments at the local, national and international level.

Mandates for Gender Equality and Equity in the Finance Sector

UN Mandates

A succession of international women's conferences organised under the auspices of the United Nations, and culminating in the Fourth World Conference on Women in Beijing in 1995, have been effective in focusing policy attention on women's needs in almost all policy areas – poverty, health, education, employment, rural development, violence etc. An examination of the Platform for Action that was ratified by governments at Beijing reveals how wide-ranging the discussion of women's interests has become. If governments are truly to implement what their delegations ratified in Beijing, this would entail significant changes in the policies, procedures, regulations and functioning of almost every ministry, as well as in the overall political and legal systems within which policy-making is embedded.

The Beijing Declaration and the Platform for Action put forward a number of strategic objectives which bear directly upon the work of Ministries of Finance, including the following (UN, 1996):

Strategic Objective A1: Review, adopt and maintain macroeconomic policies and development strategies that address the needs and efforts of women in poverty.

Strategic Objective A3: Provide women with access to savings and credit mechanisms and institutions.

Strategic Objective A4: Develop gender-based methodologies and conduct research to address the feminisation of poverty.

Strategic Objective F1: Promote women's economic rights and independence, including access to employment, appropriate working conditions and control over economic resources.

The 1995 Commonwealth Plan of Action on Gender and Development

The 1995 Commonwealth Plan of Action on Gender and Development, which was endorsed by Commonwealth Heads of Government in Auckland in 1995, gave the Commonwealth Secretariat a mandate to advise and assist governments in mainstreaming gender in all their policies, programmes and activities.

The Plan of Action identified 15 government action points as being desirable elements of national gender and development action plans, including the following:
+ integrate gender issues into all national policies, plans and programmes;

| Figure 1 | **Gender Inequality as an Efficiency Issue** |

Gender inequalities exact costs in terms of lower output, lower development of human resource capacities, and lower levels of leisure and wellbeing. If women enjoyed higher levels of economic empowerment, many countries could have some combination of greater output, greater human resource development, more leisure and greater wellbeing. Gender inequality is therefore economically inefficient.

Research on agricultural productivity in Africa shows that reducing gender inequality could significantly increase agricultural yields. For example, giving women farmers in Kenya the same level of agricultural inputs and education as men farmers could increase yields obtained by women by more than 20 per cent (Saito and Spurling, 1992).

Research on economic growth and education shows that failing to invest in education lowers Gross National Product. Everything else being equal, countries in which the ratio of female-to-male enrolment in primary or secondary education is less than 0.75 can expect levels of GNP that are roughly 25 per cent lower than countries in which there is less gender disparity in education (Hill and King, 1995.)

Research on gender inequality in the labour market shows that eliminating gender discrimination in occupation and pay could increase not only women's income, but also national income. For example, if gender inequality in the labour market in Latin America were to be eliminated, not only could women's wages rise by about 50 per cent, but national output could rise by 5 per cent (Tzannatos, 1991).

Gender inequality also reduces the productivity of the next generation - the World Bank reports mounting evidence that increases in women's wellbeing yield productivity gains in the future. The probability of children being enrolled in school increases with their mother's educational level, and extra income going to mothers has a more positive impact on household investment in nutrition, health and education of children than extra income going to fathers (World Bank, 1995).

Women's time burdens are an important constraint on growth and development – women are an over-utilised, not an under-utilised resource. The benefits of reducing this gender-based constraint can be considerable. For example, a study in Tanzania shows that reducing such constraints in a community of smallholder coffee and banana growers increases household cash incomes by 10 per cent, labour productivity by 15 per cent, and capital productivity by 44 per cent (Tibaijuka, 1994).

Research shows that gender inequality hampers a positive supply response to structural adjustment measures by reducing women's incentives to produce tradable goods and increasing women's time burdens (Brown, 1995).

Source: Elson (1996)

+ build capacity in gender planning;
+ conduct gender policy appraisal and impact assessment on macroeconomic policies;
+ implement action for women's participation in decision-making; and
+ instigate action for sustainable development, poverty alleviation and the eradication of absolute poverty.

Ministries of Finance and Gender

Despite these mandates, however, Ministries of Finance appear largely to have escaped careful scrutiny in attempts to sensitise different divisions of government to gender concerns. In gender terms, Ministries of Finance have tended to remain singularly untouched by the winds of gender change that are beginning to blow through other ministries. An examination of a range of Commonwealth Finance Ministries reveals no real attempt to consider gender at the policy level, barring the Women's Budget initiatives in Australia, Canada and, most recently, South Africa and Sri Lanka.

Nor have women's organisations in many places demanded that Finance Ministries should consider gender seriously. While women's groups have, during the Beijing conference and in different national settings, expressed considerable concern about the implications of structural adjustment reforms for women, this has generally been targeted to agencies or governments generally, not to Finance Ministries specifically (for example, see DAWN, 1995). This has been the case even though women's groups are generally aware that the lead agent of structural reforms within countries is usually the Finance Ministry.

The reasons for this yawning gap in the attempts to mainstream gender in policy-making lie in the content of what Finance Ministries do, in their prevailing ethos and attitudes, and in the relatively weak capacity of many women's organisations to engage in macroeconomic policy debates. When it comes to engendering the policies or actions of Finance Ministries, there are some inherent constraints posed by the substantive content of the work that they are expected to perform. Finance Ministries do not directly deal with people in their subject matter, but rather with monetised variables – revenues and expenditures, taxes and subsidies, allocations and appropriations. Their concerns with the budget or the aggregate money supply in the economy are by and large at the level of macroeconomic aggregates.

The impact of a Finance Ministry's actions on gender/women (or on people more generally) is felt only indirectly through the impact on macroeconomic policies and variables. This is quite different from education, health, rural development or even other so-called economic ministries such as agriculture or industry whose policies, programmes and actions directly affect the wellbeing of people. Incorporating an analysis of gender relations into the work of these ministries, while doubtless challenging, is in a sense simpler than engendering the work of Finance Ministries. Partly for this reason perhaps, there are not many Finance Ministries that have taken much action towards engendering what they do.

The content of the work of Finance Ministries also affects the ethos of the people who work there and the ambience that surrounds their work. Macroeconomics, even at its simplest, can be quite incomprehensible for non-economists or those who are not specialists in finance; it carries with it an aura of technical expertise and mystery. Those who work in Finance Ministries often come to feel themselves more powerful on the basis of superior knowledge and skills that few others can penetrate, and hence are less open to challenge by those outside the discipline.

Institutionally the Finance Ministry, especially today, is high within the pecking order of government. Working within it carries prestige and authority that social development ministries can rarely aspire to. By contrast, government institutions (whether ministries, departments, special branches or other) responsible for gender issues are often handicapped by their small size, newness, uncertain futures and poor access to resources. Although their role may include providing advice to or vetting the work of other ministries including finance, they rarely wield the institutional authority to actually do so effectively.

The barriers to engendering the work of Finance Ministries therefore include the following:
+ insufficient analytic clarity regarding the Finance Ministry's work and, in particular, its changing role during the recent period of globalisation and liberalisation of economies;

✦ the absence of a clear conceptual understanding of how gender is linked to that role;

✦ non-conducive institutional structures and ethos within which Finance Ministries function;

✦ a weak understanding of the attitudes prevalent among those who work within Finance Ministries, and how these have been changing over time; and

✦ insufficient knowledge and capacity among women's organisations to engage effectively in macroeconomic policy debates.

The responsibility for managing macroeconomic policy and setting such instruments as exchange rates and interest rates varies from country to country. In many cases, a considerable part of this responsibility lies not with the Ministry of Finance as such but rather with the Central Bank. For the purposes of this guide, the discussion of Ministries of Finance applies equally to Central Banks, and the measures suggested for engendering the Ministry of Finance can also be effective in the Central Bank of a given country.

2 The Changing Role of Ministries of Finance

Ministries of Finance Then

During much of this century prior to the 1980s, the role of Finance Ministries, while significant, was by no means pre-eminent in the development policy process. The Finance Ministry was expected to manage the government's resources through the annual budget (taxes, expenditures and transfers) so as to ensure that economic decisions taken in the planning or other ministries were financially viable. While the Finance Ministry might have urged fiscal caution in the face of over-ambitious economic plans, it rarely acted as a barrier. Indeed, many Finance Ministries in the past abrogated their cautionary role, allowing the burden of financing fiscal deficits to be passed on to the country's Central Bank. The Finance Ministry's role therefore essentially used to be a *supportive* one, and was exercised through the annual ritual of the national budget, ongoing financial approvals of detailed programmes, and monitoring of financial and monetary variables.

Finance Ministries typically functioned with relatively short time horizons, and did not concern themselves with medium or long term economic planning, which was the job of the Planning Ministry or Commission whose task was to set the long-term strategic direction for the rate of economic growth, its structure and patterns, the distribution of income and employment, the creation of physical infrastructure, human development, and poverty alleviation. In doing this the Planning Ministry co-ordinated and balanced the strategic plans of the other ministries, and worked with the Finance Ministry to ensure their financial viability.

Ministries of Finance Now

These roles and the division of labour between Finance and Planning Ministries have changed during the current period of structural adjustment-oriented economic reforms. Three factors – the end of the age of economic growth of the 1950s, 1960s and early 1970s (Howes and Singh, 1995); a major technological revolution resulting in significant changes in the structures of output and employment away from manufacturing towards services in the OECD countries; and the rapid growth and diversification of global financial transactions – have had a number of effects, including pressure for greater fiscal discipline, as well as a positive Balance of Payments in order to enable countries to compete globally while keeping inflationary pressures under control and managing external and internal debt.

Almost all countries, both high- and low-income, have faced these pressures, but for the developing countries, there has been the additional dimension of a worsened climate for development assistance. The relatively greater availability of development aid in the 1950s and 1960s had generated the belief that development resources which could not be generated internally could always be obtained through external borrowing. So-called 'aid fatigue' in the donor countries, partly the result of their own fiscal stress and growing unemployment, has increased pressure for fiscal belt-tightening, and increased export earnings to replace declining aid monies in developing countries. The fiscal stabilisation and structural adjustment packages espoused by the Bretton Woods institutions have been mechanisms to persuade governments to respond to the changed global economic realities.

The result has been a major change in the relative influence and economic clout of Finance Ministries within most countries. In a time of sharply increased fiscal stringency, the role of Finance Ministries has changed from a supportive one to a disciplining one. Planning Ministries are now required to cut their coats according to their financial cloth, and it is the Finance Ministry that determines how much cloth there is.

Ministries of Finance and Macroeconomic Management

The changed role of the Finance Ministry vis-à-vis other ministries and especially relative to the Planning Ministry and the Central Bank also reflects a major change that has occurred worldwide in the meaning and parameters of macroeconomic management. From the end of World War II to the end of the 1960s, the principal objective of short-term macroeconomic management (at least in the countries of the North) was to minimise unemployment and recessions through fine-tuning government spending and taxation. From the late 1970s onwards, however, effective macroeconomic management has meant less focus on reducing unemployment and much greater focus on inflation rates and exchange rates.

Stabilising a national economy within a liberalised global economy has meant ensuring that inflation rates remain low and exchange rates remain stable; the freedom to manoeuvre government spending so as to reduce unemployment or to pull the economy out of a recession appears to be significantly curtailed. It is within this context that one has to view the new role of Finance Ministries in relation to macroeconomic management. Maintaining fiscal discipline and strengthening the Balance of Payments is now central to macroeconomic management for which the Finance Ministry has the prime role. There are four related sets of instruments that the Finance Ministry typically uses for this purpose: the budget, the government's fiscal deficit, internal and external debt, and the Balance of Payments.

In low-income countries, structural adjustment programmes promoted by the Bretton Woods institutions have used the leverage of external debt to ensure that Finance Ministries exercise strict restraints on government deficits and on the overall budget. In practice, as is well known, the kinds of fiscal restraints adopted by some governments have had significant recessionary impacts in many countries as well as drastic cuts in public spending on both physical investment and human development.

It is arguable that, even if government expenditures have to be cut, there are different ways in which this could be accomplished. But Finance Ministries have by and large resorted to 'the politics of the squeaking wheel' in deciding where spending cuts should be made. As a result, sectors and programmes which do not have effective public 'voice' or whose beneficiaries are poor and socially disenfranchised have tended to suffer disproportionately.

Ministries of Finance and Structural Reforms

The relative weight of Ministries of Finance has changed in another important sense as well. The need to ensure greater fiscal discipline has been viewed not as a temporary result of external shocks but as more fundamentally related to poor economic management by governments. This is believed by some to have resulted in weak economic growth, excessive controls over private economic activity, curbing of economic incentives, and therefore weak capacity of the government to mobilise resources. Maintaining fiscal and monetary discipline has therefore become part of the larger structural reform process which includes: liberalising markets, limiting state economic activity, and supporting the private sector.

Ministries of Finance have come to have a key role in setting the new strategic economic directions for long-term growth. The role of Planning Ministries is now typically limited to indicative planning for long term infrastructure – both physical and human.

Along with privatisation of the public sector and of public services, the liberalisation of markets and deregulation of private economic activity are key ingredients of the current structural economic reforms supported by most Ministries of Finance. The aim of these changes is to correct biases in the allocation of economic resources that are purported to have resulted from excessive government intervention, and thereby to lay the basis for a fiscally sound pattern of economic growth and government expenditures over the medium and longer term.

Liberalisation and deregulation

Liberalisation includes a group of measures intended to raise the efficiency of resource use by removing quantitative restrictions on private investment and trade flows domestically and internationally, and reducing government controls on prices (commodities, labour, money, foreign exchange, and other services) so that prices better reflect the true scarcity values of resources. The explicitly stated intention is to remove the policy bias against the production of tradable goods, and thus to allow production to shift so that it more accurately reflects the economy's factor endowments, typically in favour of the production of labour-intensive goods for export markets. Investment, production and prices, it is argued, will thus become more closely aligned to the external sector. Deregulation is also expected to reduce wastage of resources by reducing petty corruption and exploitation at the hands of government officials, once their authority to grant permission for a range of economic activities is removed.

Privatisation

Like liberalisation, privatisation is a key ingredient of the structural reforms espoused by Ministries of Finance today. Like liberalisation, it too is expected to have both short run and medium/long term effects on the economy. The privatisation process in many countries has had two components – government divestiture from public sector enterprises, and cutbacks in government financing of public services. Each has different implications. Government sale of public sector enterprises has been viewed as necessary in order to reduce subsidies to loss-making enterprises and introduce an element of fiscal discipline. Takeovers by the private sector have usually been accompanied by labour force reductions and job losses. In some cases, public sector enterprises remain in government hands, but are encouraged to operate like private enterprises, including in their treatment of labour.

Despite the fact that, in theory at least, the main purpose of privatisation is supposed to be structural and not financial, *viz.*, changing the ownership and management structure of badly managed public enterprises, governments under severe financial pressure, have also viewed the sale of public enterprises as a mechanism for earning revenues (albeit one-off and short term only) and reducing fiscal deficits.

Actual experience with privatisation has been mixed, since the private sector is interested in buying precisely those public enterprises that have been managed well hitherto and whose books are not in the red, and not the ones that the government may be keen to get rid of. Regardless of the merits and demerits of different privatisation experiences, it is important to recognise that all three of the key ingredients of the current economic reform processes under way in many countries, *viz.*, liberalisation, deregulation and privatisation, have significant implications when viewed through a gender lens.

Liberalising credit markets[1]

In recent years, financial liberalisation and financial sector reforms have been complementary. While the former implies the removal of controls and barriers to financial intermediation including interest rate controls, the latter includes measures to improve the financial regulatory climate and strengthen financial institutions in a more liberal environment. Although such reforms are part of the larger reform process, we treat them separately here because they are directly within the purview of the Finance Ministry's and Central Banks' normal tasks and always have been.

Key aspects of financial liberalisation include changes in interest rate management practices; in the availability and distribution of credit to different sectors of the economy; in the cost of credit to different sectors particularly if credit subsidies are removed; and changes in the laws governing banks and other financial institutions.

Recent experience with financial liberalisation in a number of countries reveals both a diversification and upgrading of credit services to the higher and middle income end of the market, as well as greater integration into global financial markets, with resulting instabilities and loss of governmental control over the process. The impact on women has been mixed; on the one hand they have suffered from the reduction of credit subsidies, but on the other hand a variety of micro-credit schemes have improved women's credit access in a number of countries.

Notes

1   The discussion on credit liberalisation and financial sector reform in this guide draws extensively from Baden (1996).

3 Mainstreaming Gender in the Work of Ministries of Finance

What Does Engendering Mean?

Recent research has shown that when economic reforms are not engendered, their potential positive effects are weakened, and they have unanticipated and unplanned negative effects.[1]

The concept of engendering

By engendering we mean much more than identifying the impact of policy or programme changes on women. Engendering also involves the recognition that the gender division of labour and its associated norms, values and ideologies about masculinity and femininity are defined by a complex of power relations which tend to accord to women lesser political voice, social/cultural value, and access to and control over economic resources. These power relations of gender, while prevalent in most societies, are by no means universal in their content, and vary with historical and regional context, in addition to being crosscut by other social relations of class, caste, ethnicity, or race within a given society. Furthermore, the structures of gender power do not only define dyadic relations between women and men within a society, but can involve quite complex relations among women and among men who are at different points in their life cycles (Sen and Batliwala, 1997). Engendering policies and programmes of government ministries requires addressing these power relations in a serious way.

Engendering also implies an acknowledgement that the reproduction of human beings on a daily and/or generational basis takes resources and labour, and is mostly done outside the paid economy; its smooth functioning, however, is critical to the efficiency of the paid economy. The work entailed in human reproduction is largely done by women over and above the work they do in the paid economy. Because this work is unremunerated and often unrecognised, it imposes a variety of hidden costs on women, as well as on the growth rate of the paid economy.

Conceptually therefore, engendering a particular ministry's work requires an understanding of:

+ gender power relations and how they interact with the work of the ministry, with its institutions and structures, and with suggested policy and programme changes;

+ the implications of current and future policies and programmes on the daily and generational reproduction of human beings, i.e., on what has been called the 'care economy' (Elson, 1993) and its workers who are largely women; and

+ the impact of current policies and programmes and any suggested changes in them on different groups of women and men in terms of access, effects, etc.

This understanding can be acquired through a process of gender analysis, using gender-sensitive indicators and qualitative analyses of the relative situations of women and men both in the national economy and within the structures and institutions of government.

Engendering – practical issues

Gender mainstreaming requires a strong co-ordinated effort and the institutional means for carrying out the necessary action. The Commonwealth is promoting the Gender Management System (GMS) as a means of providing this. The GMS is defined as "a network of structures, mechanisms and processes put in place within an existing organisational framework, to guide, plan, monitor and evaluate the process of mainstreaming gender into all areas of the organisation's work, in order to achieve greater gender equality and equity within the context of sustainable development" (Commonwealth Secretariat, 1999).

Among the recommended structures of the GMS are Gender Focal Points in each ministry of government. These are designated senior members of staff who are directly involved in or able to influence their sector's planning process. They are the main agents for facilitating gender mainstreaming on a day-to-day basis within a particular ministry. In the case of larger ministries such as finance, the GMS recommends that the role of the Gender Focal Points be expanded to that of a Gender Unit consisting of several staff members who have specific expertise and/or interest in gender mainstreaming. The GMS also recommends a number of mechanisms to effect gender mainstreaming, including gender analysis, gender training and a gender-aware performance appraisal system.

Engendering Ministries of Finance

There are three possible points of entry to engendering the work of Ministries of Finance:

+ at the level of ongoing macroeconomic management which includes responsibility for the annual budget of the government and the fiscal deficit, external and internal debt, and the Balance of Payments (especially but not exclusively the capital account);

+ at the level of structural reforms intended to improve the efficiency of resource use and support poverty eradication in the economy, particularly in approaches to deregulation, liberalisation and privatisation; and

+ in the specific context of credit liberalisation and the provision of micro-credit.

These points of entry are interlinked, so that attempts to engender one area of work inevitably impinge on others. For instance, the national budget, is a key instrument not only of short-run macroeconomic management but also of the strategic reform process.

Engendering and macroeconomic management

Because of the critical linkages between short-term macroeconomic management and longer-term structural economic changes, it is important that the Finance Ministry does not take a narrow short-term approach to macroeconomic stabilisation. While ensuring fiscal and monetary discipline may be an important priority, it should not override critical requirements for a sustainable longer-term growth path for the economy. A major criticism of stabilisation reforms is that in some cases they have jeopardised the basic requirements of the growth process in terms of both physical investment and human development. A gendered approach to economic stabilisation means not only examining the welfare outcomes of policy on women and girls as compared to men and boys, but measuring their feedback effects on growth.

A key step to engendering macroeconomic management is for the ministry to conduct a *budget trade-off exercise* that will examine alternative scenarios for reducing budget deficits while strengthening the ability of government to support human reproduction needs. These needs must be seen to include aspects of human reproduction typically left out in discussions of human development which tend to focus largely on education and health, *viz.*, childcare, maternity and paternity support, safe water, and fuel, to name a few. As part of this exercise, the ministry should evaluate the opportunity cost of the possible trade-offs between a reduction in the fiscal deficit and a reduction in the potential rate of growth of the economy in the medium term, as well in the extent of poverty reduction.

Budget deficit reduction exercises under structural adjustment stabilisation are usually conducted on their own terms, i.e., in terms of what the implications of different combinations of subsidy cuts will be for the deficit itself, rather than in terms of their impact on growth or human reproduction. Typically, it has been assumed that the reduction of government expenditures will of itself release the blocks to private investment and expenditure. Experience now clearly points to the fact that private investment and markets do not automatically step into the breach when the public sector withdraws or cuts down its spending.

Furthermore actual budget cuts have often been dictated by political expediency rather than any systematic analysis. Areas of human reproduction and poverty alleviation, which do not have vocal or powerful interests supporting them, have suffered disproportionately from cuts. These areas impinge particularly on women and on gender relations since they are a key aspect of women's responsibilities. For example, there is evidence that growing pressure on adult women to earn incomes and increasing school fees and expenses has led to a greater withdrawal of girl children from school. The importance of making budget exercises more sensitive to gender concerns and to the sustainability of medium term growth cannot be stressed enough.

Engendering and structural reforms

As the key ministry directing the pace and pattern of structural economic reforms, the Finance Ministry has a critical role to play in engendering reforms even if specific decisions have to be taken by other ministries.

Liberalisation/Deregulation: The gendered implications of liberalisation measures are more clearly perceived when one examines how these measures actually work in practice. While the theory of liberalisation identifies its positive potential, there are certain caveats to be borne in mind while attempting to engender these measures.

| Figure 2 | **Tools for Engendering National Budgets** |

The Commonwealth Secretariat is developing a series of policy options for integrating gender into national budgetary policies in the context of economic reform. The policy options centre on six possible tools:

◆ **sex-disaggregated beneficiary assessments** – a research technique whereby groups of women are asked how, if they were the Minister of Finance, they would slice the national budgetary pie; the results are compared with the existing budget to see how closely it reflects women's priorities;

◆ **sex-disaggregated public expenditure incidence analysis** – this involves analysing public expenditures in such areas as health, education and agriculture to see how such expenditures benefit women and men, girls and boys to differing degrees;

◆ **a gender-aware policy evaluation of public expenditure** – evaluating the policy assumptions that underlie budgetary appropriations, to identify their likely impact on current patterns and degrees of gender differences

◆ **a gender-aware budget statement** – a modification of the Women's Budget; this is a statement from each sectoral ministry or line department on the gender implications of the budget within that sector;

◆ **sex-disaggregated analysis of the impact of the budget on time use** – this looks at the relationship between the national budget and the way time is used in households, so as to reveal the macroeconomic implications of unpaid work such as caring for the family, the sick and community members, collecting fuel and water, cooking, cleaning, teaching children and so on;

◆ **a gender-aware medium-term economic policy framework** – medium-term macroeconomic policy frameworks are currently formulated using a variety of economy-wide models which are gender-blind. Approaches for integrating gender could include: disaggregating variables by gender where applicable; introducing new variables incorporating a gender perspective; constructing new models that incorporate both national income accounts and household income accounts reflecting unpaid work; and changing underlying assumptions about the social and institutional set-up for economic planning.

Sources: Commonwealth Secretariat (1998); Elson (1996)

First, in arguing that a shift towards the production of tradables will lead to greater resource use efficiency, the theory makes an implicit assumption that international markets for most commodities are in fact competitive and therefore efficient. While this is certainly true for some markets, there is also considerable evidence that imperfect competition and oligopolistic structures dominate many international markets.

As is well known, global markets consist not of the small, perfectly competitive firms of economic theory, but of large multinational companies often operating in highly imperfect markets. In such a milieu, breaking into export markets for a small/medium producer requires pursuing one of three alternative routes – finding selective niche markets, accepting low product prices from multinational buyers, or linking up as outsourcing ancillaries to multinational producers. Among small producers, many successful exporters belong to the last category, especially in labour intensive products that rely heavily on the use of female labour. There is considerable pressure here to keep wages low, minimise benefits, and exploit gender relations to control the women workers. Furthermore, the availability of a healthy and educated female labour force is no guarantee that other cheaper sources of labour will not bid away the outsourcing firms.

In the aftermath of the ratification of the agreements creating the World Trade Organisation, a number of industrialised country governments, under pressure from their own labour organisations, have been pressing for social and environmental clauses that would give countries the right to ban the import of goods produced under 'sub-standard' labour or environmental conditions. Although most of the focus of the social clause is currently on the use of child and/or prison labour, goods produced with the cheap labour of women could also become a target.

For small firms using women's labour to be able to compete in international markets, a range of support mechanisms may be needed which involve improving the efficiency of the workers as well as marketing and input supports such as skills training, crèche services, maternity support, toilets/rest facilities. The Finance Ministry cannot focus only on keeping wages low through the standard mechanisms of labour control used in most export processing zones.

Secondly, the theory focuses on static efficiency of resource use, i.e., given certain factor endowments, the most efficient use of those resources can be made by directing production to specialise in goods using relatively more of the abundant factor. Hence economies endowed with large supplies of cheap labour are best off specialising in labour-intensive exports. But specialising according to static comparative advantage is neither necessary nor sufficient to lift an economy onto a path of high growth and structural change, as the recent experience of many East and Southeast Asian economies suggests. Static efficiency does not automatically lead to dynamic competitive advantage in global markets.

Liberalisation theory presumes that the shift of resources from non-tradables to tradables can take place relatively smoothly and quickly. In actual fact a variety of supply constraints may operate, ranging from the poor availability and quality of physical infrastructure (transport, telecommunications, corporate services) to non-availability of an experienced entrepreneurial class to the poor quality of available labour. Gender issues can constrain supply in a number of ways. In many countries, because of gender biases, lack of access to basic education or health care affects girls and women more than boys and men, making it more difficult for the former to avail themselves of new employment opportunities should they arise. Recent experience of global job creation points in fact to greater potential for female employment in labour intensive manufactures and services provided the job seekers meet basic health and education standards. This potential cannot be taken advantage of in situations where there are severe gender biases in health and education.

The gender division of labour in smallholder agriculture has also been known to constrain supply. Where women do much of the field labour but men control crop marketing and the incomes therefrom, increasing the production of cash crops means that women have to put in additional labour in cash crop fields controlled by men, over and above the labour they continue to invest in the production of food crops. If the income from increased cash cropping does not accrue to women, they cannot use it to purchase food and thereby reduce their labour in food production. As a result women have been known to be reluctant to increase the labour they invest in fields used for cash crops.

In countries where the government has played a major controlling role in the past, liberalisation tends to be confined to some sectors of the economy. These tend typically to be the large formal economy where big firms and large agricultural producers operate.

Single window permission mechanisms and simplified procedures do not appear to benefit informal sector producers and traders. This sector is one where women are heavily represented. Their efficiency continues to be hampered by exploitation at the hands of petty officials, and by traditional barriers to women's access to and control over productive assets. Land/tree rights, access to common property resources, technical services in agriculture and the self-employed sector, and a national policy in support of human reproduction can be vitally important measures.

Taken together the caveats discussed in the previous paragraphs cast some doubt on the economic efficiency of the outcomes that the theory of liberalisation predicts. The actual effects of liberalisation have in fact been rather mixed. Few countries have actually been able to raise export earnings significantly, despite removing barriers to the production of tradables. The absence in many countries of regulatory institutions appropriate to liberalised markets such as anti-trust regulatory authorities, functioning legal systems, or an effective whistle-blowing press have meant an increase rather than a reduction in political rents in many instances. In a number of countries, there has been little sign of sustained growth even in the medium term.

There have also been a number of unintended effects of doubtful value. The freeing of exchange rates and markets and the resulting movement towards world prices have led to sharp jumps in the cost of living (depending on the extent of price-cost spillovers to the domestic economy). There is now a premium on jobs which provide access to global incomes, a scramble among professionals and middle-class salary earners to obtain them, and an accelerated 'brain drain'. As economies 'adjust' to globalisation, livelihoods at the lower end of the income spectrum have become more precarious, with greater pressure on women particularly to earn incomes. Liberalisation has also meant the removal of certain types of positive discrimination, for example, low interest loans to the poor.

Addressing the gender dimensions of supply constraints, selective deregulation, imperfect competition, and industrialised country protectionism is crucial if growth is to be placed on a more sound footing. Major supply constraints such as low levels of female health, education, and lack of childcare facilities need to be addressed on a priority basis. Barriers to women's potential as producers, *viz.*, lack of land rights, or adequate access to technology, credit or other services also need to be addressed. The problems that women as informal sector producers/traders face with petty official barriers, corruption and exploitation must be dealt with so that their time and productivity can be released.

Other problems identified above are the presence of imperfect competition in global markets, and industrialised country protectionism using measures such as the 'social clause'. Neither of these is under the direct control of Finance Ministries in developing countries. However the Finance Ministry can spearhead an adequate response. Rather than reducing worker benefits in order to attract multinational capital, which often has a disproportionately large negative impact on women workers, governments should take a leaf from the book of a successful economy such as Singapore, which has concentrated on increasing worker productivity (rather than cutting costs) by raising skills, providing benefits, and thereby creating a high quality, competitive labour force, both female and male. Such a strategy would also cut the ground from under protectionist demands such as the 'social clause'.

Many of the actions to be taken under this third set of actions cannot be undertaken by the Finance Ministry in isolation. It will require it to set up a regular and *effective* institutional mechanism for interaction with other ministries under whose ambit the actions might normally fall. But the Finance Ministry needs to demonstrate the seriousness of its commitment by playing the role of nodal ministry, and spearheading the actions that need to be taken.[2]

Privatisation: For women, the public sector has been the source of some of the best paying and most secure jobs, especially in the area of services. Job reductions in this sector, therefore, tend to affect women directly by closing off one of the few avenues for better employment. Loss of jobs by male workers has also been seen to affect women as they are often expected to increase their own income-earning work to compensate for gaps in the household budget. In regions of chronic male unemployment, whether due to public or private sector job losses, field reports point to increased male alcoholism and domestic violence.

Declines in the funding of public services impinge differently on gender relations. Increased pressure to maintain fiscal discipline usually leads to intense lobbying by different economic interest groups to maintain their own share of government expenditures intact. In this political arena, sectors such as health and education have few champions, and are often the ones to suffer the most severe cuts. There is ample research that identifies the disproportionately negative effects this has on girls and women.

When schooling or healthcare access become more expensive due to cost-recovery schemes through increased user charges, societies with a preference for sons will usually cut back disproportionately on the expenditures made on daughters. More expensive or less easily accessible services means that mothers must make up for the loss through additional service provision in the home, where possible. Greater pressure on the workload of mothers usually translates into work pressure on daughters as some of the additional tasks are passed on to them. Furthermore, in the area of schooling, the effect of cutbacks has been documented in the form of higher exclusion and dropout rates, especially for girls.

In addition to cutbacks in existing services, long pending needs in the area of reproduction have tended to drop out of the public agenda. These include, for example, the need for childcare facilities among very poor women in both rural and urban areas. As economic pressure has tended to fragment extended family arrangements, and as the burden of income earning falls increasingly on mothers, childcare responsibilities often fall on older children, especially girls, thus worsening the school dropout problem. Field surveys often find household work responsibilities to be a major reason for girls dropping out of school.

Debates about the pros and cons of liberalisation, deregulation and privatisation can and ought to take better note of gender than they have to date in most countries. Certain other bases of economic identity, *viz.*, organised versus unorganised labour, small versus large producers, domestic market suppliers versus foreign traders, have been acknowledged as defining potential winners and losers as resource allocation shifts from the domestic market to tradable goods. But the potential implications of liberalisation on women as producers and managers of human reproduction need to be better recognised at the official level through support for a National Human Reproduction and Social Development Policy. There now exists a significant literature that has identified the implications of liberalisation for women in a variety of contexts. This could be drawn upon to develop a gender audit for each of the measures suggested.

Not all measures will have the same intensity of impact or even, necessarily, impact in the same direction in all countries. The components of such a gender audit would include checking for each measure, the direct and indirect impacts on different groups of women; the spillover effects to other groups, especially girl children; and the feedback effects on the rate and pattern of economic growth in the medium and longer terms.

Doing this may well require some rapid field appraisals or surveys using participatory methods.[3] A gender audit cell staffed by competent technical staff, and with direct access to the Finance Minister will need to be set up in most cases. The gender audit process should be ongoing so that the gender impact of new policy measures can be examined prior to policy decisions. Corrective measures should also be initiated on this basis.

Credit liberalisation: A major weakness of financial sector reforms is that liberalisation does not appear to reduce the fragmentation of financial markets, to the detriment of those who rely more on informal financial markets (Baden, 1996). Women typically obtain credit through such channels – family members, friends, money-lenders, chit-funds, etc., largely because of their lack of collateral and the barriers to their entry into formal credit markets. For instance, in Commonwealth countries, particularly in south Asia where a large percentage of women are still illiterate, women are unable to fill in forms or provide acceptable collateral. The micro-credit movement of recent years has attempted to address such problems so as to improve women's access to credit through the formal financial institutions. Greater awareness and support for such measures from the Finance Ministry are necessary if these improvements are to be sustainable. They need also to be linked to attempts to improve women's access to real productive assets such as land/trees/common property resources, so that their access to credit and possibility to benefit from financial sector reforms can be enhanced.

Notes

1   See for example Cagatay, Elson and Grown, 1995; Bakker, 1994; and Sen, 1996.
2   As is well-known, actions to correct gender biases often fail to fructify because of the low institutional weight of the agencies charged with carrying them out.
3   Some of the methodologies developed under the joint World Bank – NGO exercise (Structural Adjustment Programme Review Initiative, SAPRI) to study the impact of structural adjustment programmes could be adapted usefully here.

4 Institutional and Attitudinal Concerns

Promoting Attitudinal Change

Ministries of Finance hold that ensuring fiscal and monetary discipline is their overriding objective, and that liberalisation and privatisation are key mechanisms to achieve this objective. This exclusive focus on short-run macro stabilisation of economic aggregates through budgetary management seems to insulate the Finance Ministry from a need to weigh the implications of its actions for human resources development over the medium and longer terms. But the Finance Ministry in fact does a great deal more than short run macro stabilisation. It has become the key ministry setting the strategic directions for long term growth of the economy. Officers in the Finance Ministry are often reluctant to acknowledge this, and it is not hard to understand why. Long-term growth concerns more than saving, investment and other macro aggregates; it also depends on how the labour force and its capabilities, skills and expertise keep pace with the requirements of the growth process.

Acknowledging the ministry's strategic role requires therefore that the ministry begin to factor in the effects of its macroeconomic actions on the potential and current labour force, and the feedback effects therefrom to the growth potential of the economy. This has two important implications for the Finance Ministry's objective of fiscal discipline: (i) how fiscal discipline is brought about can be as important for the economy's long term growth prospects as whether it is achieved; some methods of balancing revenues and expenditures in the budget may be less damaging to human development than others; (ii) there may be trade-offs between short run fiscal stability versus medium and long-term growth possibilities; an excessive emphasis on fiscal discipline may cause serious damage to an economy's growth prospects.

Ministries of Finance cannot, in today's policy environment, concern themselves with fiscal and monetary discipline to the exclusion of the reproduction of human beings/human development that is the *sine qua non* of sustainable growth. And it is here that gender enters in a critical way. The first attitudinal shift needed among Finance Ministry officials therefore is the acknowledgement that what they do affects not only short-term macroeconomic management but the human resources needed for sustainable development.

A second important attitudinal change that is needed is about gender itself. As discussed earlier in this guide, Finance Ministry officials who are used to thinking in terms of macro financial variables, are likely to be somewhat at a loss when asked to engender their work. A change in this attitude is best likely to be effected through the process of working together with external experts on an overall framework for engendering the ministry's work.

This is likely to be more effective in sensitising Finance Ministry officials to gender than gender training that does not include a practical component. Past experience in many countries has shown that attempts to sensitise powerful government departments through gender training alone has not always been successful. Participants may tend to treat such training as a spare-time activity of little consequence to their ongoing work. For this reason, gender training within the Finance Ministry should where possible be integrated into the hands-on process of developing a gendered framework, such that officials can directly see the relevance of gender to their work; and can also themselves be involved creatively in defining how a consideration of gender will affect their policies, programmes, and work-plans.

Easing Institutional Constraints

Changing attitudes is only one of the ways in which change can be promoted within an organisational structure. Another important way is to create or support a reformation of lines of authority and incentive systems within the organisation that will make staff realise that the new directions are in their personal interest.

An important lesson that has been learned from previous attempts to mainstream gender is that the effectiveness of newly created institutions depends heavily on the extent of political will or support that they have from above, and the skill with which they can parlay this into co-operation from below. If such political commitment is not there, it often does not matter what type of institutional arrangement is made because it is unlikely to be effective. Assuming the presence of serious political support at the top levels of the Finance Ministry for engendering, the following institutional arrangements can be put in place:

+ One or two **Gender Focal Points** (individual staff members) or a special **Gender Unit** (consisting of a group of staff members), located directly in the office of the Minister of Finance or the senior bureaucrat (as appropriate), whose task would be to provide technical support for the engendering process. The role of the Gender Focal Point or Gender Unit would be to: oversee the formulation of the overall engendering framework for the ministry; support the incorporation of the framework into policies, programmes, and workplans; and identify and initiate specific research on the gender aspects of the work of the ministry. If mainstreaming of the Finance Ministry is being done in the context of the implementation of a government-wide Gender Management System (GMS), the Gender Focal Point or Gender Unit will also be represented on the GMS Inter-Ministerial Steering Committee.

+ An **inter-departmental standing committee** on gender to which senior staff from all the departments of the ministry would be seconded; the committee's task would be to develop an overall time-bound plan for engendering different aspects of the ministry's work, and to monitor and review progress. The committee should also preferably include external experts as technical advisors who would support this process.

In addition to these institutional changes, an incentive system needs to be put in place to encourage personnel to take the engendering process seriously. Innovative incentives such as an award programme (with appropriate monetary and prestige benefits) for the department that makes the most progress in engendering each year, with an external jury, could be tried. This might work more effectively than quantitative checklists whose purposes, experience has shown, are all too easy to circumvent. Other incentive systems could also be tried. For example, the GMS recommends the inclusion of gender-sensitive indicators in whatever performance appraisal system is in place in the ministry. This would include provisions for evaluating employees' performance in achieving gender goals and targets.

5 Recommendations for Action

In order to engender Ministries of Finance, a number of strategic areas of action have been identified, with specific action points in each area. These action points are not sequential in time; some of them may be undertaken simultaneously. The actual timing will vary, depending on the specific country context.

The effectiveness of the actions taken will depend in the end on the extent of political support that the process of engendering has from the highest levels of the Finance Ministry or from the Cabinet as a whole. Such support is essential to bring about the institutional and attitudinal changes that the process of engendering requires.

Strategic Areas of Action

Develop a gendered macroeconomic framework of interactions for the overall economy with particular focus on the role of the Finance Ministry

The gendered macroeconomic framework provides an analytical base for understanding gender interactions in the national context. It incorporates gender along three dimensions: gender power relations (as they impinge on the gender division of resources, labour, norms and institutions); human reproduction or what has been called the 'care economy'; and the differential impact of policies and programmes on women and girls as compared to men and boys. It would focus on three key aspects of the Finance Ministry's role: short-run macroeconomic management; setting the direction and taking key decisions regarding structural reforms; and financial sector reform/liberalisation.

Action point 1: Develop an analytical matrix

A starting point to developing the gendered macroeconomic framework is to build an analytical matrix showing the two-way interactions between various dimensions of gender differentials and the work of the Finance Ministry, as outlined in Table 1. The matrix should be developed in as much detail as possible by Finance Ministry officials with the help of gender experts. This can be done as part of a gender training programme that will provide 'hands-on' experience of considerable value. The number of rows and columns will increase as more detail is brought in. For example, in the cell on the interactions between short-run macroeconomic management and human reproduction, sub-cells might include interactions between specific elements of the budget and of aspects of reproduction such as childcare or healthcare. The specific content of the interactions in each cell and sub-cell will vary with the country context, although the broad categories of the matrix remain the same.

Table 1 **Analytical Matrix of Interactions between Gender and the Finance Ministry's Roles**

Engendering Dimensions ↓ The Finance Ministry's roles	Differential Impact on the Wellbeing of Women and Men	Human Reproduction/ the 'Care Economy'	Gender Power Relations
Short-run macroeconomic management			
Structural reforms			
Financial sector reforms/liberalisation			

Developing the gendered framework is therefore the first and most critical step; how well the framework is conceptualised will govern how effectively the next steps in the engendering process can be undertaken. The deeper the ministry's officials go into such an exercise, the more sophisticated the matrix will become and correspondingly, the better their appreciation and understanding of the importance of gender.

Developing the framework is not a one-off task to be done prior to the other steps in engendering the Finance Ministry, but an ongoing process that helps to strengthen and deepen officials' understanding of the implications of gender analysis over a period of time, for example two to three years. This process of building the framework also becomes a mechanism for maintaining substantive work and interest on gender in the ministry. It is especially important that such a framework building process be located in the Finance Ministry, because of the central and powerful role of the Finance Ministry in current structural reform processes.

An effective framework does not need to be comprehensive in the sense of spelling out all the relationships in complete detail. But at a minimum it should be developed at two levels – the aggregate economy, and the specific ministry/department's work, and it should include all three aspects of engendering. The framework should conclude with a set of guidelines that spell out how its elements can be transposed to the ongoing work of the ministry.

Once the framework has been developed, it has to be incorporated into the policies, programmes and work-plans of the ministry involved. To do this, existing policies, programmes and work-plans have to be examined in light of the framework and the points of contradiction identified. Where possible, existing programmes should be retro-fitted to bring them more into line with the framework's guidelines. This may not be feasible for all of the ministry's previously determined plans and programmes in which case some examples may be chosen for retro-fitting in order to provide lessons for future attempts.

Action point 2: Budget trade-off exercises

The budget trade-off exercises examine alternative scenarios for reducing budget deficits while supporting human reproduction needs and reducing gender inequities. Traditional budget exercises seldom take gender into account when developing alternative revenue and expenditure possibilities. Engendering budget trade-off exercises will require examining the role gender plays in the two-way impacts between annual budgets and medium- or long-term growth. Clearly, budget exercises will inform and be informed by the matrix development exercise, but they need to be seen as a distinct though linked activity.

Incorporate a gender perspective into the Finance Ministry's plans, policies and programmes

Action point 1: Gender audit

The gender audit is different from the framework building exercise in that the framework is a macro-level exercise for the economy as a whole while the gender audit is a meso-level exercise focusing on particular plans, policies and programmes. The gender audit examines how the various dimensions of gender (see Table 1 above) are affected by specific policies and programmes. It then identifies positive steps to be taken to engender these plans and programmes. The audit needs to examine ways in which the routine work of the Finance Ministry and its future plans can be made more gender-sensitive. Current programmes and plans may have to be retro-fitted to at least partly incorporate more gender-sensitive approaches.

Action point 2: National Reproduction and Social Development Policy

The Finance Ministry should take the lead in (or at least support) the formulation of a National Reproduction and Social Development Policy which would work out the modalities and financial implications of providing effective support to the 'care economy'. The Finance Ministry's task is both to work out the financial implications of different measures, and also to lend its weight and clout to the formulation of the policy.

Action point 3: Comprehensive approach to supporting women's access to assets and incomes

It is important for this effort to be spearheaded by the Finance Ministry with its standing and expertise. A key aspect of such support is ensuring women's access to credit as part of financial sector reform. Other aspects include guaranteeing women effective rights to land, trees and common property resources; promoting availability of technology and training for women particularly in agriculture, small scale industry, and self-employed services; the removal of gender inequitable practices in labour markets (unequal wages, occupational segregation, sexual harassment/violence); and the removal of barriers to self-employment by women. While many such measures fall within the purview of other ministries, the Finance Ministry can help by working out their financial costs and benefits from the viewpoint of the overall economy, and also provide its support to less powerful ministries.

Address institutional and attitudinal concerns

Action point 1: 'Hands-on' approach to gender training

Moving the engendering agenda forward in a ministry as powerful and complex as finance requires a strong institutional structure. Much of the work required to be done will be quite new to the ministry's officials, and an appropriate institutional set-up needs to use external gender expertise judiciously as well as draw out the knowledge and co-operation of the ministry's own experts. The action points suggested above provide the opportunity for a hands-on approach to gender training, one which involves finance ministry officials in the development of the gendered framework, the gender audit, and gender-sensitive policies.

Action point 2: Establish institutional arrangements

The setting up of a technically competent gender focal points or a Gender Unit in a strategic location in the office of the Minister of Finance or senior bureaucrat is an important institutional arrangement for gender mainstreaming. The Gender Focal Point or Gender Unit, which should be staffed by people with expertise in both macroeconomics and gender, would backstop the activities in the first two Strategic Areas, initiate research to fill in knowledge and data gaps, draw on the expertise of external consultants as needed, and liaise with counterparts in other ministries. The competence, tough-mindedness, and tenacity of the Gender Focal Point or Gender Unit are key ingredients in an effective engendering strategy.

Since many of the proposed measures and actions cross over the different departments within the Finance Ministry (revenue, taxation, etc.), an inter-departmental standing committee may also be necessary. The function of this committee is to facilitate communication and co-ordination across all departments. The overall engendering strategy of the government may also require a high-level inter-ministerial standing committee that would draw up plans, and monitor and review the progress made. The Gender Focal Point or the head of the Gender Unit in each ministry, including the Ministry of Finance, would be the representative on the inter-ministerial steering committee.

Action point 3: Incentives and disincentives

The structures of incentives and authority within the ministry/department need to be examined and modified to ensure that the engendering is successful. This is the critical step between the theory of engendering and its actually being put into practice. It involves a set of actions that challenge entrenched interests and ways of doing things within the ministry/department itself. Carrying out this change requires, therefore, the strongest possible support from the highest level of the ministry (or even beyond), in order to overcome possible inertia, resistance, or even outright opposition.

A system of incentives and disincentives needs to be developed so that Finance Ministry officials and employees find it in their interest to take gender seriously. Measures that are more creative than the traditional checklists need to be developed. For example, performance appraisal systems could be updated to include references to established gender targets and achievements, and to the level of gender awareness attained by employees. Since these measures may not be specific to the finance ministry alone, developing them may be one of the first tasks of the inter-ministerial steering committee, with technical back-up from the Gender Unit in the Finance Ministry. Ideally, such incentives should be put in place by the government's central personnel office or Public Service Commission, as part of an overall strategy for gender mainstreaming.

References

Baden, S (1996). "Gender Issues in Financial Liberalisation and Financial Sector Reform". Topic paper prepared for the Directorate General for Development (DGVIII) of the European Commission.

Bakker, I (ed.) (1994). *The Strategic Silence: Gender and Economic Policy*. London: Zed Books.

Boserup, E (1970). *Women's Role in Economic Development*. New York: St Martin's Press.

Brown, L (1995). *Gender and the Implementation of Structural Adjustment in Africa: Examining the Micro-Meso-Macro Linkages*. International Food Policy Research Institute: Washington DC.

Budlender, D; Sharp, R and Allen, K (1980). *How to Do a Gender-Sensitive Budget Analysis: Contemporary Research and Practice*. Canberra and London: Australian Agency for International Development and the Commonwealth Secretariat.

Cagatay, N; Elson, D and Grown, C (eds.) (1995). *Gender, Adjustment and Macroeconomics*. Special Issue of *World Development* 23:11.

Commonwealth Secretariat (1998). *Gender Mainstreaming: Commonwealth Strategies on Politics, Macroeconomics and Human Rights*. London: Commonwealth Secretariat.

Commonwealth Secretariat (1999). *Gender Management System Handbook. Gender Management System Series*. London: Commonwealth Secretariat.

DAWN (1995). *Markers on the Way: The DAWN Debates on Alternative Development* (DAWN's Platform for the Fourth World Conference on Women, Beijing).

Elson, D (1993). "Gender-Aware Analysis and Development Economics". *Journal of International Development* 5, 2: 237-247.

Elson, D (1996). "Integrating Gender Issues into National Budgetary Policies and Procedures within the Context of Economic Reform: Some Policy Options". Paper prepared for the Commonwealth Secretariat, Fifth Meeting of Commonwealth Ministers Responsible for Women's Affairs, Port of Spain, Trinidad and Tobago, November 1996.

Hill, A and King, E (1995). "Women's Education and Economic Wellbeing". *Feminist Economics* 1, 2: 21-46.

Howes, C and Singh, A (1995). "Long-Term Trends in the World Economy: The Gender Dimension". *World Development* 23, 1: 1895-1912.

Saito, K and Spurling, D (1992). *Developing Agricultural Extension for Women Farmers*. World Bank Discussion Paper 156, Washington, DC.

Sen, G (1996). "Gender, Markets and States: A Selective Review and Research Agenda". *World Development* 24: 5 : 821-829.

Sen, G and Batliwala, S (1997) "Empowering Women for Reproductive Rights: Moving Beyond Cairo". Paper presented at the seminar on Female Empowerment and Demographic Processes: IUSSP, Lund.

Tibaijuka, A (1994). "The Cost of Differential Gender Roles in African Agriculture: A Case Study of Smallholder Banana-Coffee Farms in the Kagera Region, Tanzania". *Journal of Agricultural Economics* 45, 1: 1-4.

Tzannatos, Z (1991). "Potential Gains From the Elimination of Gender Differentials in the Labour Market", in George Psacharopoulos and Zafiris Tzannatos (eds.). *Women's Employment and Pay in Latin America*. Report No. 10. Latin America and Caribbean Technical Department. World Bank: Washington DC.

UN (1996). *The Beijing Declaration and the Platform for Action: Fourth World Conference on Women, Beijing, China, 4-15 September 1995*. New York: United Nations.

UNDP (1997). *Human Development Report 1997*. New York: United Nations Development Programme.

World Bank (1995). *Towards Gender Equality: The Role of Public Policy*. Washington DC.